MW00411737

In Praise of
MOMS

In Praise of
MOMS

Edited by Mary Carnahan

Illustrations by Eliza Gran

Ariel Books

Andrews McMeel
Publishing

Kansas City

www.andrewsmcmeel.com

ISBN: 0-8362-6800-8
Library of Congress Catalog Card Number: 98-84241

Contents

Introduction

There is no job more important in the world than that of raising children well. From the first sense of a life growing within, through birth, the early years, the pitfalls and pratfalls of pre-teen and teenage years, and young adulthood, mothers, in a sense, reinvent the wheel. All the little things add up: how to tie shoelaces, to dress, to color, and to brush teeth; how to explore a book, to argue, and to joke. The smallest lessons planted inside a child bear fruit years later.

Mothers instill an appreciation for life and love and friendship, foster individuality and responsibility, and cook meals with that special touch. Years after children leave to make their own lives, snatches of childhood songs come to mind, and the feel of a soft blanket or the smell of Mom's perfume will trigger a sweet moment of remembrance.

Moms hold and rock, feed, change diapers, pick out new school outfits, set limits, and worry. Motherly pride and protectiveness are acknowledged in every culture. The passing of years changes the issues, but

not the basic job: to care, and
care deeply. Friendship, advice,
and tolerance are the basic
building blocks of every person,
and mothers, more than anyone
else, are the keepers of these
qualities.

The Power of Motherhood

Oh what a power is motherhood, possessing a potent spell.

—EURIPIDES

No event ever in my life has been so profound, so joyful, so moving. I fell in love as I never have before or since.

—ALI MACGRAW

Sometimes the strength of motherhood is greater than natural laws.

—BARBARA KINGSOLVER

She broke the bread into two fragments and gave them to the children, who ate with avidity. "She hath kept none for herself," grumbled the Sergeant. "Because she is not hungry," said a soldier. "Because she is a mother," said the Sergeant.

—Victor Hugo

The thorn from the bush one has planted, nourished, and pruned pricks most deeply and draws more blood.

—MAYA ANGELOU

The baby has learned to know and love you better than anyone else and now he wants you all the time and all to himself. . . . His ideal would be your continual presence and constant attention.

—PENELOPE LEACH

Motherhood is still the biggest gamble in the world. It is the glorious life force. It's huge and scary—it's an act of infinite optimism.

—Gilda Radner

Probably there is nothing in human nature more resonant with charges than the flow of energy between two biologically alike bodies, one of which has lain in amniotic bliss inside the other, one of which has labored to give birth to the

other. The materials are here
for the deepest mutuality and
the most painful estrangement.

—ADRIENNE RICH

You almost died," a nurse
told her. But that was nonsense.
Of course she wouldn't have
died; she had children. When
you have children, you're obli-
gated to live.

—ANNE TYLER

A mother is not a person to lean on but a person to make leaning unnecessary.

—DOROTHY CANFIELD FISHER

Because I am a mother, I am capable of being shocked: as I never was when I was not one.

—MARGARET ATWOOD

We are transfused into our children, and . . . feel more keenly for them than for ourselves.

—MARIE DE SÉVIGNÉ

When God thought of Mother, he must have laughed with satisfaction, and framed it quickly—so rich, so deep, so divine, so full of soul, power, and beauty, was the conception.

—HENRY WARD BEECHER

Romance fails us and so do friendships, but the relationship of parent and child, less noisy than all others, remains indelible and indestructible, the strongest relationship on earth.

—THEODOR REIK

In the sheltered simplicity of the first days after a baby is born, one sees again the magical closed circle, the miraculous sense of two people existing only for each other.

—ANNE MORROW LINDBERGH

Most mothers are instinctive philosophers.

—HARRIET BEECHER STOWE

Templeton," said Wilbur, "if you weren't so dopey, you would have noticed that Charlotte has made an egg sac. She is going to become a mother. For your information, there are five hundred and fourteen eggs in that peachy little sac."

—E. B. WHITE

Charlotte's Web

There is no influence so
powerful as that of the mother.

—SARAH JOSEPHA HALE

Youth fades; love droops;
  the leaves of friend-
  ship fall:
A mother's secret love
  outlives them all.

—OLIVER WENDELL HOLMES

Making the decision to have a child—it's momentous. It is to decide forever to have your heart go walking around outside your body.

—ELIZABETH STONE

A mother is a person who, seeing there are only four pieces of pie for five people, promptly announces she never did care for pie.

—TENNEVA JORDAN

There is nothing so strong as the force of love; there is no love so forcible as the love of an affectionate mother to her natural child.

—Elizabeth Grymeston

There is an amazed curiosity in every young mother. It is strangely miraculous to see and to hold a living being formed within oneself and issued forth from oneself.

—SIMONE DE BEAUVOIR

Claudia . . . remembered that when she'd had her first baby she had realized with astonishment that the perfect couple consisted of a mother and child and not, as she had always supposed, a man and woman.

—ALICE THOMAS ELLIS
The Other Side of the Fire

I had a baby. He was beautiful and mine. Totally mine. No one had bought him for me.

—Maya Angelou

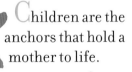

Children are the anchors that hold a mother to life.

—Sophocles

Being a mother, as far as I can tell, is a constantly evolving process of adapting to the needs of your child while also changing and growing as a person in your own right.

—DEBORAH INSEL

A mother's arms are made of tenderness and children sleep soundly in them.

—VICTOR HUGO

A Mother's Job
Is Never Done

By and large, mothers and housewives are the only work- ers who do not have regular time off. They are the great vacationless class.

—MADELEINE L'ENGLE

I looked on child rearing not only as a work of love and duty but as a profession that was fully as interesting and challenging as any honorable profession in the world and one that demanded the best that I could bring to it.

—ROSE KENNEDY

A woman who can cope with the terrible twos can cope with anything.

—JUDITH CLABES

The phrase "working mother" is redundant.

—JANE SELLMAN

God could not be every-
where and therefore he made
mothers.

—JEWISH PROVERB

I figure if the kids are alive
at the end of the day, I've done
my job.

—ROSEANNE

Mother—that was the bank where we deposited all our hurts and worries.

—T. DeWitt Talmage

If motherhood is an occupation which is critically important to society the way we say it is, then there should be a mother's bill of rights.

—BARBARA ANN MIKULSKI

There is no such thing as a nonworking mother.

—HESTER MUNDIS

She had found that the more the child demanded of her, the more she had to give. Strength came up in waves that had their source in a sea of calm and un-conquerable devotion. The child's holy trust made her open her eyes, and she took stock of herself and found that everything was all right, and that she could meet what challenges arose and meet them

well, and that she had nothing
to apologize for—on the con-
trary, she had every reason to
rejoice.

—MAEVE BRENNAN

Mothers . . . are the first
book read, the last put aside in
every child's library.

—C. LENOX REMOND

When people ask me what I do, I always say I am a mother first. Your children represent your thoughts. Your children are a statement.

—JACQUELINE JACKSON

It's not easy being a mother. If it were, fathers would do it.

—DOROTHY OF *The Golden Girls*

The mother loves her child most divinely, not when she surrounds him with comfort and anticipates his wants, but when she resolutely holds him to the highest standards and is content with nothing less than his best.

—HAMILTON WRIGHT MABIE

Mothers have to handle all kinds of situations. When presented with the new baby brother he said he wanted, the toddler told his mother, "I changed my mind."

—JUDITH VIORST

The mother is the most precious possession of the nation, so precious that society advances its highest well-being when it protects the functions of the mother.

—ELLEN KEY

W ho will speak for the bride
but her mother?

—Egyptian proverb

When you are a mother, you are never really alone in your thoughts. You are connected to your child and to all those who touch your lives. A mother always has to think twice, once for herself and once for her child.

—SOPHIA LOREN

The mother-child relationship is paradoxical and, in a
sense, tragic. It requires the
most intense love on the
mother's side, yet this very love
must help the child grow away
from the mother and become
fully independent.

—ERICH FROMM

Raising children is far more creative than most jobs around for men and women.

—BENJAMIN SPOCK

Though motherhood is the most important of all the professions—requiring more knowledge than any other department in human affairs—there was no attention given to preparation for this office.

—Elizabeth Cady Stanton

I long to put the experience of fifty years at once into your young lives, to give you at once the key of that treasure chamber, every gem of which has cost me tears and struggles and prayers, but you must work for these inward treasures yourselves.

—HARRIET BEECHER STOWE

Anyone who thinks mother love is as soft and golden-eyed as a purring cat should see a cat defending her kittens.

—PAM BROWN

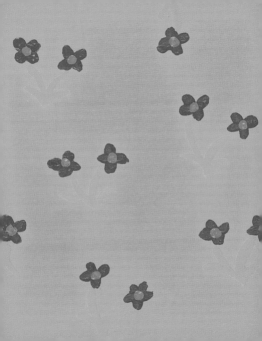

Memories
of Mom

My mother made a brilliant impression upon my childhood life. She shone for me like the evening star—I loved her dearly. . . .

—WINSTON CHURCHILL

The heart of a mother is a deep abyss at the bottom of which you will always discover forgiveness.

—HONORÉ DE BALZAC

Mama exhorted her children at every opportunity to "jump at de sun." We might not land on the sun, but at least we would get off the ground.

—ZORA NEALE HURSTON

I grew up believing that
there was nothing, literally
nothing my mother couldn't do
once she set her mind to it. . . .
So in a way when . . . the
women's movement happened,
I was really delighted because I
felt they were trying to go where
my mother was and where I always assumed I would go.

—ALICE WALKER

My mother wanted me
to be her wings, to fly as she
never quite had the courage
to do. I love her for that. I
love the fact that she wanted
to give birth to her own
wings.

—ERICA JONG

I cannot forget my mother. Though not as sturdy as others, she is my bridge. When I needed to get across, she steadied herself long enough for me to run across safely.

—RENITA WEEMS

The essential thing about mothers—one needs to know that they are there, particularly at that age when, paradoxically, one is trying so hard to break away from parental influence.

—MARGOT FONTEYN

I was kind of a mama's boy until I was twenty-one.

—Woody Harrelson

My mother used to say, "Watch yourself. The higher you are, the farther you can fall. Never let pride be your guiding principle. Pride itself. Let your accomplishments speak for you."

—Morgan Freeman

Who is it that loves me and will love me forever with an affection which no chance, no misery, no crime of mine can do away?—It is you, my mother.

—THOMAS CARLYLE

It was my mother who taught us to stand up to our problems, not only in the world around us but in ourselves.

—DOROTHY PITMAN HUGHES

My mother was not just an interesting person, she was interested.

—JOYCE MAYNARD

If it had not been for my mother's conviction and determination that music was my destiny, it is quite conceivable that I would have become a carpenter.

—PABLO CASALS

When my mom got really mad, she would say, "Your butt is my meat." Not a particularly attractive phrase. And I always wondered, "Now, what wine goes with that?"

—PAULA POUNDSTONE

No man is poor who has had a godly mother.

—ABRAHAM LINCOLN

My mother was the source
from which I derived the guiding principles of my life.

—John Wesley

My mother [Tippi Hedren]
raised me to be independent—
as she is. Hitchcock gave her an
ultimatum: Go to bed with him
or he'd ruin her career. "Ruin
it," Mom said.

—Melanie Griffith